The Rough Draft of My Life Story

The Rough Draft of My Life Story

written by Andrew Lapham Fersch
illustrated by Phillip Ashworth

Alright I'm Wrong *press*

The Rough Draft of My Life Story
Copyright © 2011 by Alright I'm Wrong

Library of Congress Catalog Card Number: 2011919053
ISBN 9780615553665

For You

Rude Raymond Pettigrew

Rude Raymond Pettigrew

Look how he grew

Then, one day

He split into two

And two days later

From two he turned into four

And after two more days

He became four more

And that eight became sixteen

And two more passed by

And that sixteen thirty two

Oh heavens, oh my

And it might not bother you that much

If eventually

He was 22,222 plus two

Well, it would be

Quite bothersome

If he didn't like you!

The Screaming Eagle

I'm flying so fast, all feathers and talons, right at you

You freeze, eyes open wide, with no idea what to do

I scream, 'BACKAW!' flapping my wings wildly to fly

You fall down, pointing and laughing so hard that you cry

They're all here!

An army of ants

a sleuth of bears

a smack of jellyfish

a husk of hares

a rhumba of rattlesnakes

a sounder of swine

an unkindness of ravens

a prickle of porcupines

a rookery of penguins

a wisdom of wombats

a cackle of hyenas

and a cluster of cats

every single one -

surrounding me

Ø Ø Sandwich

There he was

That small, smelly sandwich

Hiding on a shelf

Sitting there silently

Surveying the scene

Smiling suspiciously...

Spying on me

Karma

I stepped on an ant
     and ended its life
I laughed out loud
     not considering his children, his wife
Someone must have been upset with what I had done
And thought turning the tables might be sorta fun
For a second I laughed
     being small was really neat
But that didn't last long
     when I saw huge ant feet

All That I Need

I'm not tall enough (I'm six inches too short)

I have a boring house (I'd rather live in a fort)

I've got three friends (I'd rather have four)

My toy collection would be perfect (if I just had one more)

That double in baseball (was not a home run)

That roller coaster was decent (but the line wasn't fun)

My clothes don't have holes (but they certainly aren't new)

My legs and arms aren't weak (but I'm weaker than you)

I'd go play in the sun (but there's a bit of a breeze)

And I'd go lay on the beach (but the sun makes me sneeze)

But then I looked 'round, and I had a strange thought

And realized just how many good things I've got

If I didn't use my time to complain and to whine

Maybe everything in life would be just fine

Enough dissatisfaction, enough of my greed

I realized, in my life, I've got more than I need!

King Wrigley the VIIIth

I'm the bubblegum king

Everyone else is an imposter

If you had a bubblegum team

I'd be the MVP of your roster

Chewing fifteen pieces of every single brand

You can't even hold that much gum in your hand

Brands that no longer exist, on them I'm still chewing away

I've already had seventy-two pieces of Fruit Stripe today

Don't be sad or ashamed though

It's not a skill that has served me well

Since I'm writing this (I forget to mention)

On a desk, right here, in detention

Bartholomew Bartleby

Bartholomew Bartleby loves climbing trees

Bartholomew Bartleby just found out he's allergic to bees

Car For Sale,
For Sale
Real Cheap

It was the cheapest car for sale on the lot

And I asked many questions before I bought

Right before I paid, the salesman said, "No refunds"

And looked like he was trying to hide a smile

I should have thought twice when I saw that

But I hadn't met a salesman in quite a while

I handed over my hard-earned dough

And his smile got bigger, and he counted it slow,

"Well, congrats, you're the owner of this very nice car

Let me just explain, before you drive off too far

Something I forgot to mention real quick

This car doesn't run on gas, and it's not electric

It's a pretty simple fuel, no whistles or bells

The car you now own runs on terrible smells

Yup, you heard right, get ready to stink

Terrible smells aren't strong fuel, as one might think

If you want to get to the beach, you'll need moldy fruit

And if you want to go to the store

You'll need some rotten milk and an unwashed cowboy boot

Want to go farther? The smells must be stronger

To get good mileage with your fuel

The smell must stay in your car longer

Two hours or more requires ten pounds of wet dog fur

And to go somewhere four hours away

You'll need a very used diaper

By the look on your face, I can tell you're afraid

I wouldn't bother with that, you've already paid

So good luck with your car, I'm sure it'll work just fine

All I can say is that I'm glad it's not mine!"

The Surprise Prize in the Bottom of the Box

The prize in the bottom of the box

Of Berry Blast Bran Bunches

Was something magnificent

(Said one of my hunches)

And when I got there

After three bowls a day

I was sorely disappointed

(That's the least I can say)

For this tiny plastic spaceship, all covered in Bran dust

Was no better than an old nail, all covered in brown rust

Then something caught my eyes, a tiny direction

Which read, 'Read carefully, for your protection

This toy is no, but needs water to grow

And it will take a while for the watering to show

Make sure you place it in a field, give it a few drops a day

And right after you feed it, promptly run away

And within two weeks, if you follow these rules

(And aren't convinced we're lying, like so many fools)

You'll have the greatest cereal box treasure, of all time, of ever

You'll no longer be bored, not soon, no not never!'

Intrigued, I followed these peculiar rules to a T

Excited by the prospects of what I might see

And after one day, there was no change

And after one week, nothing seemed strange

And I started to believe that it was all just a lie

But I'm no fool, so I gave two weeks a try

And on the fourteenth day, after watering and running away

Something wild happened, much too wild to say

I do wish I could see the look on your face

As you read this transmission I sent from Outer Space

Broccoli Dan & Cauliflower Joe

"Cauliflower Joe,

What the cauliflower do you know?"

Mocked Broccoli Dan

From inside his old one-windowed van,

"You're pale and white

And ugly as sin

And no one'd miss you

If they never saw you ag'in!

You've got no taste in music of clothes

And you've got something hanging

From your nose

You make girls scream

And you always smell

But now I'm going,

So oh well."

"I know one thing," said Joe

A smile on his cauliflower face

"That you can't catch me

Even at my slowest pace."

Broccoli Dan laughed, "I've got this van!"

"Without this key, drive it if you can!"

And off ran Cauliflower Joe

Laughing at Broccoli Dan.

Henri

Inspired by Kaci West

Your eyes closed, your breathing did deepen

And around your room, I got a-creepin'

I opened your dresser and swam in your clothes

I had to jump out, the smell hurt my nose

They splashed on the floor, and I must confess

Just that alone made a pretty big mess

Then I opened your chest with your favorite toys

And battled them all, and made lots of noise

Yet your eyes stayed closed, and asleep you did stay

I kept a-walking around, and continued to play

Your crayons drew a masterpiece on your wall

And with your model plane, I played basketball

I took your shoelaces and tied them all

And fashioned a trip wire out in the hall

Next your baseball cards, I threw them about

Tap-danced on your homework as I started to shout

By then I was tired, so I climbed back in bed

And curled up, smiling, right next to your head

In the morning: a shout in the hall, your door slammed open

And I knew you were in for it, just like I was a-hopin'

You didn't kiss me goodnight, and that's just *not* okay

I was excited to hear what your mother would say

And she shouted, "What on Earth happened here!?"

You looked all around in confusion and fear

Then confusion disappeared, your eyes focused on me,

"I'm not to blame mom, it must have been Henri!"

The look on her face wasn't amused, not even a bit,

"Don't blame Henri, he's a stuffed animal, he's inanimate!"

The Rough Draft of My Life Story

I picked up my pen to start to my life story
And I wrote that I had been a dare-devil
I jumped on a plane, skydived into Spain
And took my motorcycle out in the rain

I wrote down that I traveled the world
Walked with a panda along the Great Wall of China
Trekked to Antarctica and back
And then stopped over in France, for an afternoon snack

I added in that I was an artist
Painted a landscape, recorded a song
(Tried my hand at poetry – but not for that long)

I was a family man, filled with gratitude and joy
With a beautiful daughter, so sweet, kind, and free
And an amazing wife I still can't believe chose me

And I looked at a story I thought had written me
And I smile a big, broad, glorious smile
Realizing I had written it, and because of that
I got to be everything I wanted to be

Two Peas in a Pod

We were so close

      We turned into two peas in a pod

Considering yesterday we were people

      That does seem quite odd

Now we roll around town

      And have so much fun

And return to our pod together

      When we are done

The Sink Stops Stink

Inspired by Zeb Raszmann

My mom didn't want me to stink
so she had me bathe in the sink
I was on the left, toys on the right
That bath was the best part of every night

And it may seem odd to you
that it's still what I choose to do
I just don't seem to fit so well anymore
now that I am forty-four!

Ham vs. Spam

(vs. Mr. Leonard Skinner)

There was Ham

And there was Spam

Got in a brawl

In the hall

Over a call

In gym

Ham couldn't throw a pitch

no arms

Spam wouldn't have been able to swing either way

So Mr. Skinner said they were both to blame

and threw both of them out of the game

The fight didn't last long

it didn't matter that they were both strong

All they could do was bump into each other, nothing more

and it wasn't long before they both fell over and were trapped on the floor

Then Mr. Skinner walked by

and there was a hungry look in his eye

and a roll in his hand

I do! You don't!

I do!

You don't

You can't

I **won't!**

Just did

No way!

For sure

So you *say*

Chocolate Cake for Breakfast?

My dad made a funny voice
And told me to eat chocolate cake
(For breakfast nonetheless!)
He encouraged me to be sloppy
And not to clean up my mess!
I'll never know why he was
Surprised, but I believe
His response was unfounded
It certainly wasn't a funny voice
That he used, when he shouted,
"You're grounded!"

I'm The Monster Under Your Bed

I couldn't hide in your closet

Your closet was locked

I couldn't turn off your lights

Your light switch wouldn't switch

And scaring is this job's only perk

I wonder if I'm cut out for this kind of work

I waited for hours in the washer

After seeing your filthy pile of clothes

Thinking you'd *have* to put them in

I know I would, but with you, who knows!

And when I heard those footsteps

I started to beam

It just wasn't the same, terrifying your mom

She doesn't have that great of a scream

What kind of monster has this much

Trouble scaring a small child?

I'm at the end of my wit!

You know what? I quit!

Strike Against Hunger

I ate three sandwiches

Two pizzas

One Coke

Four cookies

Five milkshakes

I don't know how much more I can take!

I figured you'd change your mind

    and buy me a new bike

As a result of your concern about my health

    during my hunger strike

It's not working, but why, maybe I'm doing it wrong

If I keep my hunger strike going, it won't even matter

I'll be too big to ride a bike before long!

The End of the Rainbow

It was raining so I stuck out my tongue

To catch some drops

All of a sudden, the sun comes out

The raining stops

And a rainbow flew directly from my mouth

And into the sky

And then a Leprechaun

Came strolling by

Asked him for his pot of gold

But when I spoke the rainbow, it just left

Gone, without a trace

And I was standing there, quite bereft

And the small man in the green suit

Looked at me, angry and forlorn

Shook his head in disgust

And rode away on his unicorn

Second Place Steve

Hot dog eating contests
aren't all that much fun
when you always enter
and you've never won

I've Got This Disease

This disease I've got wasn't always this bad

If you can believe it, there was a day when I was entirely mad!

And then I saw you, and I started to smile

And that was something that lasted a while

I waved to you, you came over and said "Hi"

Your kindness and sweetness made me no longer shy

So we got to talking and took a stroll

The pleasure of each other's company our only goal

Then you said something clever and also quite cute

And intelligent and sweet, and very astute

For some reason that smile, it turned into a laugh

And I realized right then that I am only a half

Together with you I am complete and I'm whole

And maybe this happy disease, is life's only real goal

Half a giraffe

I'm only half a giraffe
as you can see
I'm not sure how I'm telling you this though
There's no head on me

The Super Duper Spectacular Amazing Glorious Bicycle

I've invented a bicycle that goes faster than a plane

and is more comfortable than the most comfortable luxury train

and yes, it flies, and can go in the sea

sure, it can become invisible if you're trying to find me

It's invincible like a super hero, and strong as an ox

And only works when I ride it, it doesn't need any locks

It's bright red, and shiny, you can't help but look

It's smart too, knows how to read and it has read *every* book

It tells the best jokes, makes me laugh so hard

and it's stronger than you, my personal body guard

There's just one little fact I managed to omit

I haven't yet figured out how to actually build it!

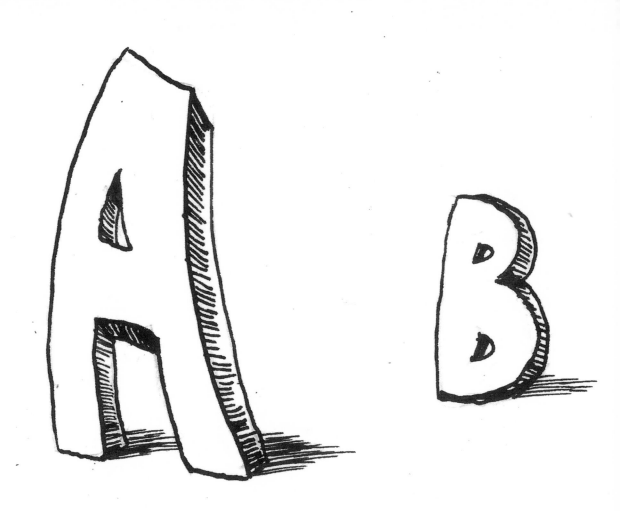

Alphabet Stu

I'm Alphabet Stu
and I'm A for Amazing…
what are you?

Hide and Go Emu

I'm an emu

who, unbeknownst to you

is playing hide and go seek in your shoe...

BOO!

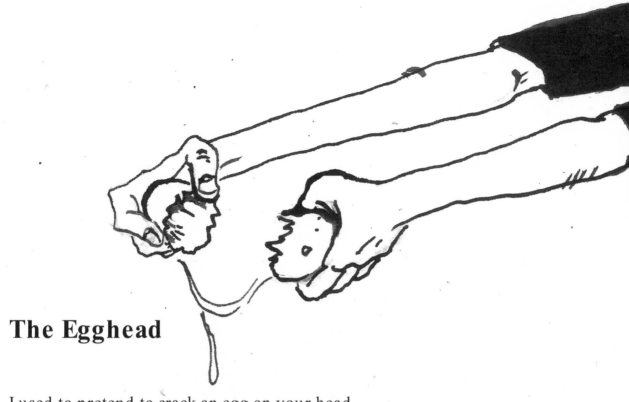

The Egghead

I used to pretend to crack an egg on your head

And you'd laugh, and shiver, and say 'That's not real, nice try'

When you said that today, all I could do was stare

The difference is, today you've got an egg in your hair!

Free Hugs, Hugs For Free,
Come On Someone,
Get Over Here And Hug Me

I love a good hug

it makes me feel warm inside

If I said I'm not addicted

you'd be right that I lied

For some reason though

it's been quite a while

since I got my last hug

I'm a sad croc-o-dile

My Wallet

That lemur, that one right there

Yeah that one with the ring tail, the very dark hair

Who is frolicking, playing, having such fun

Lounging on his back, basking in the glory of the sun

Who looks so cuddly and so very sweet

Adorableness that really just cannot be beat

Yeah, that one:

he stole my wallet.

_ ___'_ _____ (I Can't Talk)

I'm writing this down

on a piece of paper

because I lost my voice

when I held my breath

in a contest with my brother

and even though I ended up finding it

I'm not allowed to talk

because, even though I didn't mean to

and I thought it would be a whisper

when I was explaining why I was so angry

I yelled at my mother

Eye See Something

Inspired by Kimberly Morse

It was mid-August, one of those beautiful nights

The only light in the sky were the moon and street lights

So we played some catch, and we played some tag

Even some truth or dare, and some capture the flag

And we were out of ideas for what to do

But it was as if someone else already knew

Because the lights began to flicker, turning off and on

One second they'd be bright, the next, all light was gone

They danced with precision, but we knew not why

Till something in the distance, it caught my eye

It was a saucer, a flying one too

I hollered, "If it can do this, what else can it do!?"

And so we ran off in terror, and so very afraid

Completely forgetting about all the games we had played

And made it to our house, safe, at least for now

We told our folks the story, all they could say was 'Wow'

Then my mom looked in my eyes and she looked a little blurry,

"I'm not so sure that either of you should worry."

It might not have been aliens

I really can't say

Because as my mom pointed out

I wasn't wearing my glasses today

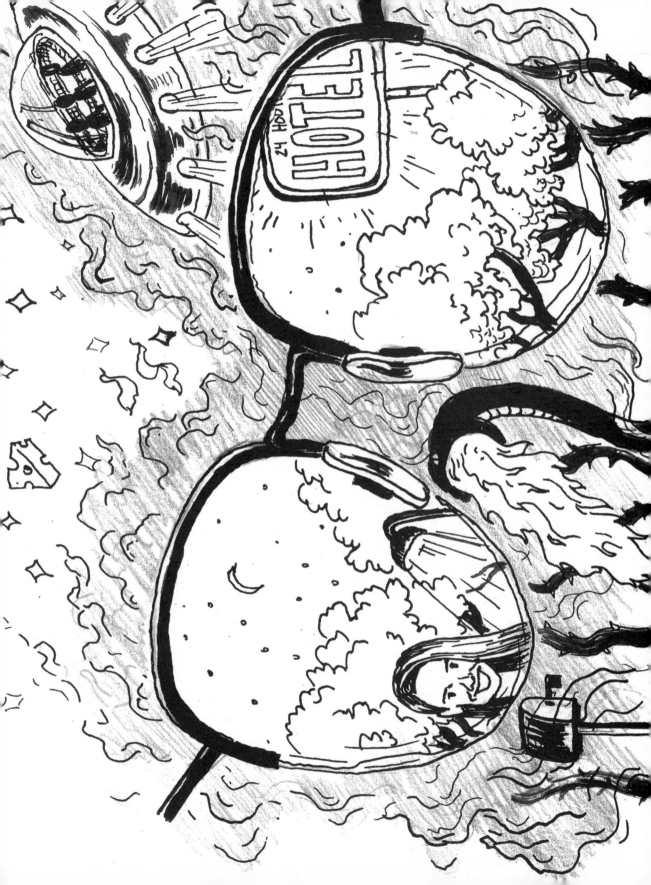

Phil Fell Flat

Phil fell flat

Fell flat on his face

When he tripped on his way

On his way to home base

And Chuck should have changed

Should have changed his speedy pace

For base running in baseball isn't

Isn't always a race

And so after rounding

After rounding third base

He crashed into Phil

KA-BOOM!

And both of them crumbled

Crumbled like a fragile vase

It wasn't a good way to lose

And boy did they lose

Without any grace

The World's Greatest Dive

The stairs were steep

The water deep

This was a promise that I could keep

I climbed up slow

To put on a show

And at the top I was ready to go

I got to the edge

Of that ultra-high ledge

And slipped....

What was meant to be the world's best dive

Turned into an ugly hop

And suddenly I was about to do

The world's greatest belly flop

Franklin Frances Ferdinand

Franklin Frances Ferdinand walked around on his knees

Franklin Frances Ferdinand is now all covered in fleas

Backwards With Time

Inspired by Scott and Seth Avett

Ug built a time machine in 200,000 BC

And what did he do with it? He visited me!

At first I was shocked it wasn't the other way 'round

Then he started to talk and my jaw hit the ground,

"Kind sir, I do hope that I do not intrude

And apologies if you find my unexpected visit rude

I just wanted to see what the future would be,"

And then he explained why he chose to visit me,

"See, I'm your great, great, great, great, very great grandpa

And considering how intelligent our family is

I wanted to see how important we became

If we didn't do something spectacular, it would be a shame!"

I was at quite a loss with what to say

so I just gave him a quick synopsis of my typical day,

"Well, I'm usually up by noon, I've been unemployed since May

I was dating someone, but they left me today

I've got no friends, I didn't make it through school

I'm not much to look at, and I still think I'm cool."

As I spoke, his face filled with such fright

And he said, "Oh dear, I must bid you goodnight,

Hurry back to my time, and chat with my son

See if there's anything that can be done

For it really should be considered a crime

If our family manages to grow backwards with time!"

And as he left, through lights all shiny and bright

Disappearing right before my very eyes into the past

I got to thinking; I wonder what's on TV?

All Tied Up

I tied my shoes

I tied a record

I tied my tie

I think I'm a pretty smart guy!

Hire Me, I'll Work For Free!

I said I'd be willing to babysit for free

I figured the children would do my work for me

Instead, they stole my clothes, money, and tied me to a chair

And left me there, embarrassed, in my underwear

I'd quit this job but I don't actually get paid, and chances are

If I tried to escape, these little monsters wouldn't let me get very far

When I Escape From This Jail

When I escape from this jail

I know what I'll do

I'll hotwire a car

And come visit you

I'll run every red light

Swerve over the yellow line

When I get pulled over

I'll pretend everything is fine

Lie to the officer

Maybe lift his wallet too

Then I'll spit out some gum

To get stuck to his shoe

Then I'll speed

Right over to your place

I'll probably tear up

When I see your face

If I escape from this jail

That's exactly what I'd do

If I knew how to break out

So I could come and visit you

You Made Me, Me

Trying to be you

I found myself being him

Trying to be him

I found myself being Jim

While being Jim

I began to walk faster

And soon I was Sam

A karate master

My playing a bassoon

Made me Kate

And then I started being a baboon

Because of all the bananas I ate

And my love of climbing trees

Made me Kelly

Falling down, I skinned my knee

Called out to my mommy

And she made me, me

The Angry Anteater

Antonio Anteater is hungry
And wants food
But he can't eat
So he's always in a terrible mood
It's not that there aren't tons of ants
From which to pick
It just so happens
That he's allergic

Yes, it's true, I'm cooler than you

Yes, it's true

I'm cooler than you

I cut my shirt short

I've got a band in my head

And I'm jumping up and down

On my brother's bed

Don't be upset

By my unique clothes

Or the fact that I'm not afraid

That my personality shows

Cause I know who I am

And I'm proud of it too

Do you think you could say

The same thing about you?

Sloppy Sally and Clean-Up Carl

Sally drops her ice cream on the floor

Along with pickles and pears

And leaves a terrible mess

Up and down the stairs

She tracks in dirt and mud

Drops cake on the rug

Refuses to wash herself

And always spills from her mug

Carl sweeps and Carl complains

(But never really means it)

Sally makes more messes and Sally says sorry

(But never really cleans it)

64

I Moo, How 'Bout You?

I *moo*, how 'bout you?

I *backaw*, and it just won't do!

Well, I *baaah*, with no feeling in my voice

I'd rather do that than *chirp*, if I had a choice

I have an idea then, why don't we just trade?

And they did, and for a while

Were happy with the changes they made

Now I'm the only cow that goes *chirp*

And I'm the only eagle that goes *moo*

No other chick can *baaah*

And a *backaw* from a sheep? That's something new!

Yet it didn't feel right

Something was most certainly wrong

I'm being given a hard time for being different

Was the choice we made wrong?

So they talked and they thought

And argued and fought

And decided to return to their natural sound

With this trade, something more important was found

It isn't the noise that makes me, me

It's what I have to say, don't you all see?

So whether I *backaw*, *baah*, *chirp*, or *moo*

Being myself is all I really need to do

The Follower

"I don't feel like doing much of anything," you say,
"How could I want to on such a rainy day?
I will not jump in puddles
Till the puddles are gone
I will not run out the door
And slide 'cross the lawn
I will not dance a dance
I will not sing a tune
I will not run around
hollering like a buffoon."

"Well if you won't join me
That's your loss not mine
Because to have no shadow follow me today
Sounds perfectly fine!"

It's Empty

It's empty, no thoughts
no kind and no mean
It's hollow, no feeling
ears with nothing between

I'm blank, at a loss
I've got nothing to say
I guess that's enough
trying to think for today

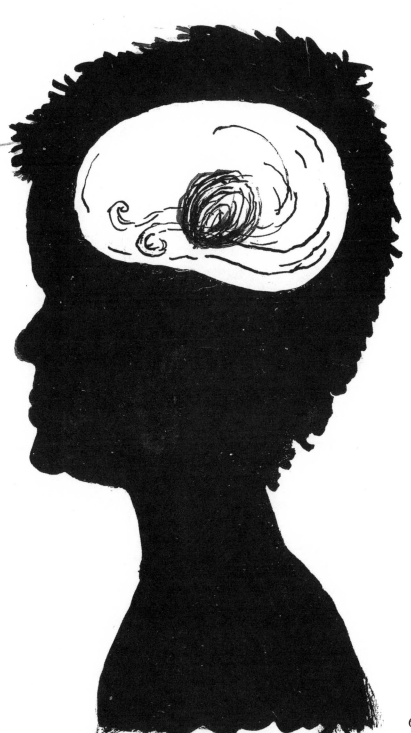

My names for you

I called you fat, you said I was flat

I called you tall, you said I was small

I called you too clean

You called me too dirty

I called you too quiet

You called me too wordy

Together we realized we had a new favorite game

and that other than looks, we're exactly the same

Eat Your Greens

My mom told me, "Eat your greens, big and strong you'll grow"

Well here's what really happened (shows you how much she knows)

I ate all my broccoli, asked for seconds on peas

I was tired of being eye level with everyone else's knees

I felt something happen, and started to think mom was right

I could barely sleep, I was so filled with excitement that night

When I woke, I looked at myself in the mirror on the on the wall

And guess what? I'd shrunk, I wasn't growing tall!

My face grew as red as the tomato I'd made myself eat

And I knew that was a mistake I wouldn't soon repeat

So I went to the kitchen, opened the cupboard door

And took out all of the chocolate, brown sugar, frosting and more

And ate until I couldn't move

At dinner, the greens were given to our loyal dog Buddy

While mom thought I was following her advice, she couldn't see

Can you believe that? She trusted me!

And I kept sneaking in the kitchen, and kept hoping I'd grow

It wasn't very long before my hopes started to show

My smile was as tall as I started to be

Yet for some reason, mom seemed concerned about me,

"Something's wrong, you aren't growing the right way

What exactly was it that you ate today?"

I admitted that for weeks I'd be sneaking treats

But she shouldn't be mad

I was growing! They couldn't be all bad

She brought me into my room and asked me to show her

How I was measuring my height

With a proud smile on my face, I showed her

I stood in front of the mirror, and she let out a sigh

She turned the mirror and told me to take another look

I was in shock, for the mirror had lied

I hadn't grown tall, I'd grown wide!

Hornswaggled!

It was an absurd plan

A boondoggle some would say

That would hopefully be serendipitous

(Having pizzazz either way)

We would bombard and hornswaggle the guards

In a tizzy we would deliver them

With gobbledygook and flummery

Our factotum would then swipe the gem

They'll be awestruck by our genius

A scuttlebutt will ensue

And thanks to my skills as a raconteur

Everyone will blame it all on you

My Above Ground Whale

Lounging in the pool I thought I was safe

On an inflatable shark, enjoying the sun

All of a sudden I started to feel something move

Little did I know what has just begun

The shark was real,

"Tricked you, right? Now I'll eat you!"

The trick was on the shark

because the pool was a whale pretending too

I'm not sure though

if you could say that I won

although it is interesting

     Living inside of a whale

      Hanging out with a shark

I probably wouldn't call it fun

The Cards

The cards you were dealt

don't decide the game

And your life won't be ruled

by your last name

So be the best that you

can possibly be

And do it for yourself

don't do it for me

Chop, Chop, I Chop

Inspired by Jeff Marks

Chop, chop, I chop

in my butcher shop

and the pig says hi

the cow says bye

the chicken takes your money

and the lamb tells jokes

(which can sometimes be funny)

So then what do I

chop, chop, I chop

in my butcher shop?

Juicy apples

sweet potatoes

large pineapples

and ripe tomatoes

I couldn't hurt a friend

and vegetables are my foes

so here, animals

needn't feel any woes

because I know

that although we have to eat

here I butcher vegetables

and am friends with the meat

78

The Whiner

I broke my knee, I have to pee

When I took a hike, guess what fell on me? A tree

My clothes are gnawed by moths, my haircut is just bad

And you know who just went to jail? My dad

I cheated on a test, got caught and expelled

You should have heard how loud my mom yelled

I smell quite bad and I can barely see

I bet you think I'm a whiner; you'd be too if you were me!

Left-Handed Lou and
Right-Handed Ralph

The ball went flying over the fence

And Left-Handed Lou picked it up and threw

And it rolled directly to the feet

Of Right-Handed Ralph, who gave a frown, and yelled,

"Hey Lou, you throw like a clown!"

Lou stopped in his track, and his lip curled

As he whispered, "At least *I* can play first base."

Right-Handed Ralph threw the ball on the ground

And ran over to Left-Handed Lou

"How dare you mumble under your breath at me

I've had enough of you!"

And Ralph shoved Lou, which Lou knew he'd do

And Lou had to let him know he knew that fact too

Right-Handed Ralph walked away

Angry and sure he was right

Left-Handed Lou walked away

Blaming only Ralph for the fight

The most unfortunate fact

About them getting in each other's way

Is that, even if they're a little different

By yourself, there aren't many games you can play

The Lark and the Hornet

Inspired by Shannon Owen

Mother nature

Gave me my stinger to sting

And gave the lark

A beautiful voice to sing

To me, that decision

Well, it doesn't seem quite fair

I don't want to cause pain

I'd rather be kind and share

So I'm going on a strike from stinging

I don't care what you say

And I'm flying on down to sign up

For voice lessons today

I'm
Already
Asleep

I turned off the lights

When you sent me to sleep

For being rude to you and dad

I hadn't done a single thing wrong

How dare you punish me!

I was seething mad

And I heard you come to the door

So I closed my eyes tight

Pretending I was already asleep

You sighed a deep sigh

Kissed me on the forehead and left

And I started to weep

I ran into your room

And all you did was open your arms wide

It's no use pretending I could stay mad at you

Even if I tried

Vote for ME!

"Vote for ME!

Sammy Smith for student council Prez!"

Sammy shouted, riding in a small car

As she donned an oversized fez

I'll put a soda machine in the Caf

And in-between classes

I'll tell jokes over the intercom to make you all laugh

I'll hire a personal chef at lunch, no more Sloppy Joes

Tired of walking? A private masseuse for all

To massage your ankles and toes

You'll get no homework, only teachers do

And if they don't finish it, they'll apologize to you

Recess will be thirty minutes (with an additional hour or three)

And you can spend that in the gym or art room

Or a giant hot air balloon, exploring the world with me

School will be cancelled if there's snow or wind or rain
Sun or birds chirping, or there's fresh air to breathe
Does this sound good? Or too good to believe?

Only one way to find out, vote for ME!
Sammy Smith, and you'll see!

Make Your Bed!

The grass is taller than a giraffe standing up

There are no clean dishes, not a single clean cup

My bedroom floor is covered with dirty clothes

And there's so much grime you can't see out the windows

My friends are going swimming in the lake

     And they want me to join too

That doesn't look so promising with mom yelling,

    "You've got chores to do!"

Suzanna Serena Southworth

Suzanna Serena Southworth was in the shed, looking behind the rakes

Now Suzanna Serena Southworth has been eaten by snakes

Nothing Is Much Fun

I poured tea in two cups, then drank too much tea

I went skydiving alone, no one saw it but me

I measured my height against just my own on the wall

After each throw in catch, I had to run after the ball

I had a thumb war alone and I still managed to lose

I'm Sherlock with no Watson, searching for clues

I lost the three-legged race, I only have two

Nothing is much fun, unless I get to do it with you

In The Land of Dreams

My eyes they close as my body does doze

I start to breathe deep, then I snore; I'm asleep

There are pirates, unicorns, spiders, and magic

Most dreams are quite nice, some are awfully tragic

The worlds I feel are so vivid and real

So memorable and amazing, I really must say

Nothing like this happens during my day

Yet when I awake, the memories, they all go away

Why Don't You Act Your Age?

"Why don't you grow up
And act your age?"
He said to the girl
Who said not a word

"And while you're at it
Why don't you wear normal clothes?
And stop with the wild colors
Painted on your fingernails and toes

"Now that we're on the topic
Show some respect to your elders
And look at me when I'm speaking to you
Has no one ever told you what to do?

"Stop smiling so much, life is tough
And stop asking for more
You have more than enough

"And stop laughing so loud
And don't you sin
And by being too proud
By looking for attention."

Then up she got

A broad smile on her face

Her hair and clothes weren't what was out of place

And gave him a kiss on his cheek,

"Thanks for your advice

How about I be who I am

And you who you are

Wouldn't that make this world so nice?"

And she skipped away

A smile on her face, a laugh in her heart

And in his way of living

She'd take no part

92

McKinley
Marston
Mumford

McKinley Marston Mumford went swimming in the sea

McKinley Marston Mumford was soon thereafter mangled by manatees

Telephony

Eyeball glue

   eyeball goo

      I fall who?

         I call moo

            Aye, crawl too

               Aye, cry to

                  Eye lie two

                     Aye live new

                        I love you

Funambulism

I'm not much for heights

Large crowds I do not like

I'm allergic to rope

And I've disliked elephants

Since I was a tyke

So why, might you inquire

   am I the star of the

    one man tight rope walking show?

Well, it's a fantastic and interesting story

    let me tell you...

     Noooooo.......

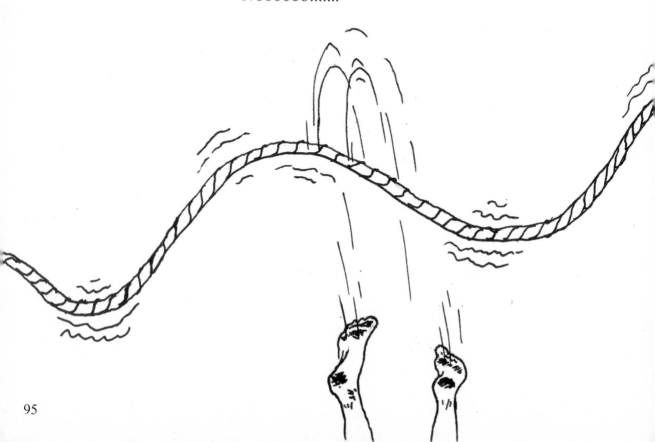

All you need is patients

went to the kitchen and took out the flower

know that baking takes patients

don't want anything to go to waist

mixed together leak, chilly, and karats

Added locks, chocolate moose, and time

t all looked pretty grate

And when it was all done, I sat down and eight

Tiny Voice Tony

The World's Quietest Traffic Cop

I'm the world's quietest traffic cop

All day, at the top of my lungs, I shout **stop**!

But as you can clearly see

no one is able to hear me.

Whineasaurus Rex

I don't want to go to the beach

I don't want pizza for dinner

I don't want to watch a movie or the TV

I don't want to do my homework

I don't want to go on a hike

I don't want to bake cookies

And I don't want to ride my new bike

I want the exact opposite of

Everything you are offering me

How much easier could that possibly be!?

Tomato, potato, butternut squash

Tomato, potato

Butternut squash and rhubarb

Mustard greens, kidney beans

Jalapeno and nettles

Broccoli, celery

Asparagus and radicchio

I don't like any of you

I just thought you should know!

I'm Supposed To

Happy Birthday to you?

How about Happy Birthday to me?!

I'm two minutes older

     which means two minutes smarter

     two minutes more cool

     two minutes better

So let's celebrate me for now

     and if we have time, we'll get to you

Please try not to be too upset

     this is what big brothers are supposed to do!

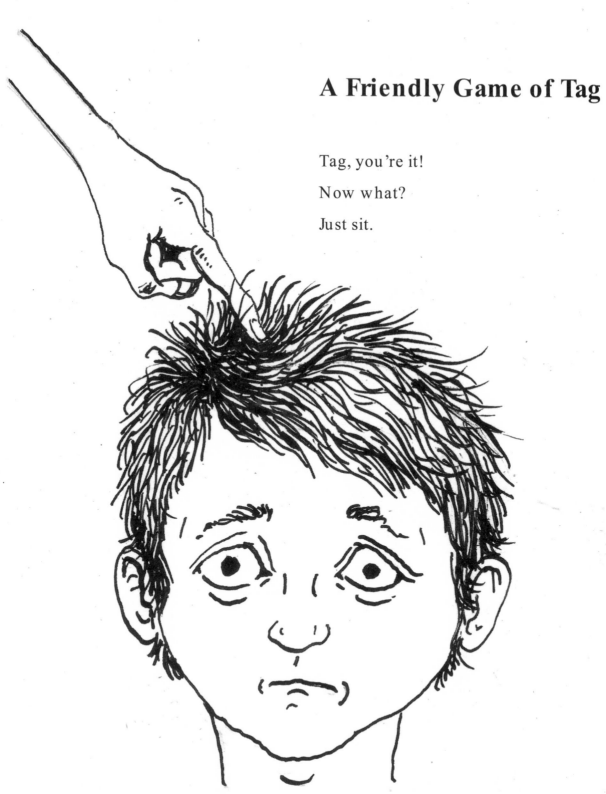

A Friendly Game of Tag

Tag, you're it!

Now what?

Just sit.

Munjoy Hill

Pedal fast

Picking up speed

Until I hit Munjoy Hill

And the pedaling slows

And my legs

Start to kill

And it's all worth it

Once I make it to the top

And stop, look around

And admire the view

All the while knowing

Exactly what I'll do

I turn my bicycle around

And start to smile

It *Would* Be So Quiet

It's so quiet you can hear a mouse scurry

It's so quiet you can hear a feather float

It's so quiet you can hear a cotton ball squish

It's so quiet you can hear a pin drop

Well, it *would* be so quiet

If your talking would just stop!

The Ballerina

Around and around I find myself turning

bobbing up and down with the song I always hear

And no matter how far you sometimes feel

I always dance when you are near

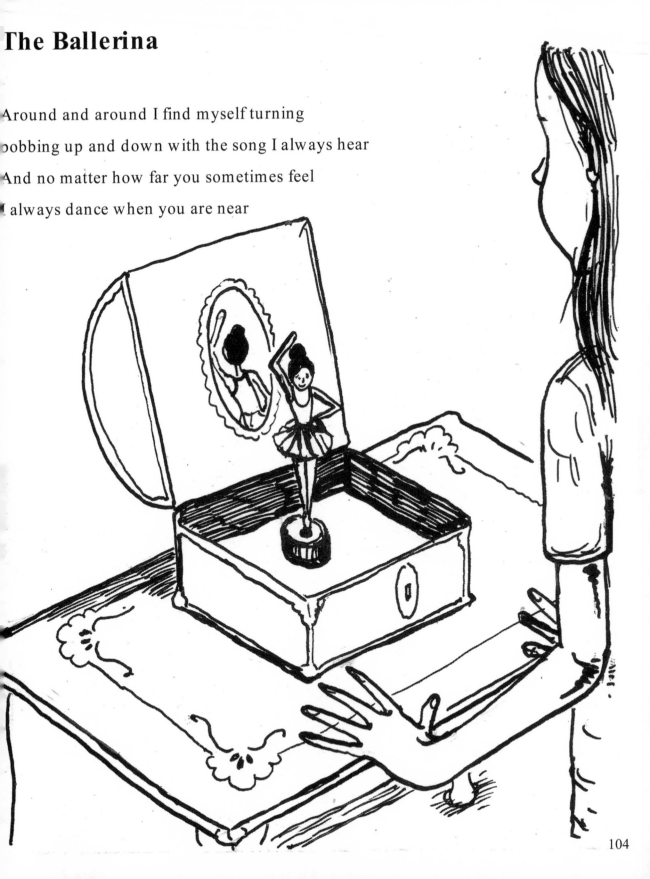

The Road Less Traveled

Our car is trapped in this traffic jam

And I'd like to be anywhere but here

So I closed my eyes, and thought real deep

Before I knew it, off I fell, sound asleep

The car grew wings and up I flew

And I was up with the birds before I knew

Up there, there was so much smog though

That I headed to above where even birds can't go

Then a terrible noise and racket

Scared me half to death

After that a plane nearly hit me

It took quite a while to catch my breath

So further up and up I went

To where the atmosphere's thin and it's hard to breathe

And it seemed that peace had found me at last

Until a space shuttle thundered past

And in my dream, I closed my eyes

And I thought real deep

I thought about us, and the noise we make

And all the things for granted we take

At the next exit, off the highway I sped

And followed the road less traveled

To see where it led

The Family Pet

All of my pets have been on a leash

     My dog, my iguana, even my cat

So I just figured you put a leash on something

     It becomes your pet, simple as that

And when mom and dad got home

     And were so furious with me

I tried to explain that I'd fed my pet, given him water

I even let him go to the bathroom

     On the neighbor's lawn

They yelled and said I was grounded

     All my privileges gone

When I asked why they were so shocked, my father shouted,

     "You put a leash on your five year old brother John!"

Dirty Dan and Smelly Sue

Dirty Dan and Smelly Sue

Always tell me what to do

'Get out of our way' and

'Watch what you say' and

'My, don't you look awful today'

I'll hold the door, and offer them a snack

And all the while, they remain on the attack

'You aren't very cool' and

'You dress like a fool' and

'I bet you wake up all covered in drool'

And I would be mad

If they both weren't so sad

And got more attention from their mom and their dad

And so to their confused faces, I always say

I hope that you have a wonderful day.'

My Secret Fort

In the deepest and darkest part of the forest

Where no one dares travel

There is a notch in a tall oak tree

   That you'd never notice, unless you were me

And this notch means that two branches up

   (And one to the right)

Is the branch you must reach

   (And pull with all of your might)

And from the ground will rise a small stump

   (Jump on it fast or lose your chance)

And when you get on top of it

   It's time for your most entertaining and energetic dance

The hidden camera will pass that on to me

   (And then assuming I like what I see)

A 50 foot rope will drop down that you must climb

   And will bring you face to face with the ruler of this land

And then in your kindest voice

   Ask to see my fort, pretty, pretty please

And maybe if you beg, down on your knees

   I'll say yes

But probably not

My Flag

My flag has many symbols

No single one more valuable than the next

A box of Kleenex

Emotions are alright, go ahead and let them out

A multi-colored slinky

Be flexible (and look cool while doing it)

A cold pizza being put into a microwave

Don't be wasteful, especially when it comes to pizza

A hippopotamus

Even things that seem harmless totally want to eat you sometimes

A broken down car

Don't rely on technology (too much)

A rack of ribs

Ribs are delicious and I had them for dinner last night

An astronaut's helmet

Explore the world, there's some neat stuff out there

There were more -

But I went exploring in Africa

A hippo charged me and knocked some of the symbols off my flag

That's when I added him to it

So maybe that is more valuable than the rest

INDEX

All That I Need, 17-18
All Tied Up, 57
All You Need Is Patients, 96
Alphabet Stu, 43
Angry Anteater, 62

Backwards With Time, 55-56
Ballerina, 104
Bartholomew Bartleby, 20
Broccoli Dan, 25-26

Cards, 75-76
Car For Sale, 21-22
Chocolate Cake for Breakfast, 35
Chop, Chop, 77-78

Dirty Dan and Smelly Sue, 108
Double 0 Sandwich, 15

Eat Your Greens, 71-72
Egghead, 45
End of the Rainbow, 38
Eye See Something, 49-50

Family Pet, 107
Follower, 67
Franklin Frances Ferdinand, 54
Free Hugs, 46
Friendly Game of Tag, 101
Funambulism, 95

Half a Giraffe, 41
Ham vs. Spam, 33
Henri, 27-28
Hide and Go Emu, 44
Hire Me, 58
Hornswaggled, 73

I Can't Talk, 48
I Do, You Don't, 34
I'm Already Asleep, 84
I Moo, How 'Bout You, 65-66
I'm Supposed To, 100
In The Land of Dreams, 90
It's Empty, 68
It Would Be So Quiet, 103
I've Got This Disease, 40

Karma, 16
King Wrigley, 19

Lark and the Hornet, 83
Left-Handed Lou, 81-82

Make Your Bed, 87
McKinley Marston Mumford, 93
Monster Under Your Bed, 36
Munjoy Hill, 102
My Above Ground Whale, 74
My Flag, 111-112
My Names For You, 69-70
My Secret Fort, 109-110
My Wallet, 47

Nothing Is Much Fun, 89

Phil Fell Flat, 51-52

Road Less Traveled, 105-106
Rough Draft of My Life Story, 29-30
Rude Raymond Pettigrew, 12

Screaming Eagle, 13
Second Place Steve, 39
Sink Stops Stink, 32
Sloppy Sally and Clean Up Carl, 64
Strike Against Hunger, 37
Super Duper Bicycle, 42
Surprise Prize, 23-24
Suzanna Serena Southworth, 88

Telephony, 94
They're All Here, 14
Tiny Voice Tony, 97
Tomato, Potato, 99
Two Peas in a Pod, 31

Vote For Me, 85-86

When I Escape From This Jail, 59-60
Whineasaurus Rex, 98
Whiner, 79-80
Why Don't You Act Your Age, 91-92
World's Greatest Dive, 53

Yes It's True, 63
You Made Me, Me, 61

For his unwavering support in all things, my most sincere thanks to my father. For my mother, who helped me become me. And for my brother. Thanks to Phil Ashworth; I'm fortunate to work with someone so talented. Thanks to Nora Sørena Casey; your input and ideas were truly invaluable. Thanks to TJ Metcalfe and Courtney Graf. Thanks to Rolf, Mr. Roof, and Shel for being wonderful teachers. And to all the students who supported and encouraged me over the last few years with my writing, especially Chelsey and the Consortium, who were there at the beginning and the end.

Thank you for reading.

My Wallet:

The Whiner:

1.

Rough Draft for my life story:

- All in pencil
- un-inked image
- or beginning to be inked?
- imply a work in-progress.

It's Empty:

2.

3.

It (would be) so quiet!

Monster faces:

2) Tiny Voice Tony:

61.) Funambulism

62.) Franklin Frances....

63.) Already Asleep.

64.) Greatest Dive

65.) My name's for you

66.) Mckinley Murston...

67.) Suzanna Sandra....

PHILLIP ASHWORTH is a graduate of the Rhode Island School of Design, Phil now works out of Brooklyn, NY and hopes that he can be paid to draw forever, but will continue to draw even if this is not the case. He also rides his skateboard every day even though he is a grown man. He enjoys these two things the most, but also enjoys the company of cats, camping, watching the sun set from his roof, movie marathons, and seeing kids still playing outside. You can see more of his work/reach him at: www.philashworth.blogspot.com

ANDREW LAPHAM FERSCH is a teacher first and a writer second (but don't worry, he still puts a lot of love into his writing). He spends his free time writing, cooking, riding his bicycle, and listening to music. His poetry can be found at: www.AndrewFersch.com. He can be reached at: onehundredyears@gmail.com.